CONTENTS

AWAKENING: ONE MAN'S JOURNEY TO FIND PURPOSE IN A DIVIDED COUNTRY

JOSH Z.

INTRODUCTION

There are moments in life that shift the ground beneath our feet, moments that force us to see the world in a new light, whether we want to or not. For Hank Ellis, a blue-collar worker from a small Southern town, that moment came unexpectedly. It didn't happen overnight; it was a gradual pull, a feeling in his gut that something was off, that there were questions left unasked, answers left unsaid.

Hank had spent his life working hard, providing for his family, and believing in the systems that were supposed to serve him. He trusted the news, voted in every election, and figured that if he kept his head down and did what he was supposed to, things would work out. But as the years went on, he found himself struggling more, questioning more, wondering if he'd been living under an illusion.

One late night of reading led to another, and soon Hank found himself on a path he hadn't planned. A path that questioned everything he thought he knew. This book is his story, a story about what it means to wake up to a new reality, to search for answers that often seem elusive, and to wrestle with the cost of that search. It's a story of truth, purpose, and the delicate balance between seeking answers and holding on to the things that matter most.

Hank's journey is one that many will recognize, whether they've taken it themselves or watched a loved one take it. It's a journey that asks us all to look within, to question not just the world around us, but the beliefs that shape us, the connections that sustain us, and the sacrifices we're willing to make in pursuit of meaning. This is Hank's story—but it's also a reminder that the search for truth is one we all share.

CHAPTER 1: THE OLD FAMILIAR PATH

My name's Hank Ellis, fifty-four years old and a welder by trade. I've lived in this town my whole life, and my work shows in half the buildings around here. I like to think I'm someone who knows the meaning of a hard day's work, of seeing something tangible come out of the hours I put in. A few years back, I could have sworn I'd be working in this place till I retired, just like my dad did before me. That's how we all thought things would go. Folks here don't dream big—we just dream simple. A steady paycheck, a home we can hold onto, and maybe a little extra to send the kids to college or take a vacation down to the beach every now and then. Nothing flashy. Just decent.

Growing up, my dad taught me about respect and loyalty—to my family, my town, and my country. He was a proud Democrat, and it rubbed off on me. I remember listening to him talk about people like FDR and JFK, how they cared about the "working man." He'd tell me stories about the Great Depression, how FDR's programs put food on the table for families like ours. "Democrats look out for the little guy," he'd say, a certainty in his voice. And for most of my life, I didn't question that belief. It just was.

By the time 2016 rolled around, it felt natural to vote Democrat. I didn't know much about Hillary Clinton besides what I'd seen on the news, but she seemed like a safe choice, a familiar name. Donald Trump, though... he was a wild card. The guy was a millionaire reality star, famous for his buildings and his bluster. His whole "Make America Great Again" campaign seemed like a joke to me. Why would someone who'd spent his life in penthouses and TV studios understand anything about folks who have to work for a living? Back then, I didn't buy what he was selling.

But then he lost, and I thought that would be the end of it. The country would go on, things would settle, and we'd forget about all that noise. Yet here we are, years later, and I don't know if I've ever felt more uncertain about this country. Somewhere along the line, it feels like something broke, and I can't tell if it's the country, the politics, or just me.

These days, nothing feels steady. Gas prices climb. Groceries are sky-high. I work the same hours I did a decade ago, but my paycheck seems to shrink every month. My wife Lucy and I sit down to pay the bills, and it's like we're racing just to keep up. We can't afford the same things we used to, and I know it's not just us —most folks around here are feeling the same pinch. I can see it on the faces of the guys I work with, in the way they hold back on the little luxuries they used to enjoy.

One day, I stood by the welding rig, talking to my buddy Joe during a break. We talked about everything and nothing—the weather, the cost of living, how things "just ain't right" anymore. He shook his head, hands rough and cracked from years of labor.

"It's like they don't care about us anymore, Hank. We're just cogs in the machine, and they keep turning up the pressure till we break."

I nodded, feeling the weight of his words settle into my bones. It's one thing to read about numbers and statistics, but it's another thing entirely when you're the one living through it. The gap between what they said on the news about a "booming economy" and what I saw around me grew wider every day. It made me wonder, made me question if the "American Dream" was even something we could hold onto anymore.

That night, as I sat on our old couch, I thought back to the election, to how I'd laughed at Trump's slogans and promises. Back then, I'd figured he was just out for himself, that he'd get bored and move on. But even with him out of office, it felt like his words still lingered. His talk about a "swamp" and a rigged system... I'd dismissed it all as theatrics, but now I wasn't so sure. Maybe there was something there I hadn't seen before.

When Lucy got home, I mentioned some of my thoughts, hoping she might feel the same way. She looked at me, a little surprised, before nodding slowly.

"It's not just you, Hank," she said, her voice low and tired. "Feels like every time I go to the grocery store, something else has doubled in price. They say it's all under control, but it sure doesn't feel that way."

She was right. The headlines were full of reassurances, claiming things were stable, that the "data" showed progress. But I wasn't seeing it, and neither was anyone I knew. I couldn't put my finger on it, but there was a sense, deep in my gut, that we were being left behind, sacrificed on some invisible altar of progress that didn't include us.

As the days wore on, I started paying closer attention. The same news anchors, the same politicians, they all repeated the same lines. "Things are improving. The economy is strong." Yet my bank account told a different story, and so did the lives of people around me. I began to wonder—who was benefiting from all this "progress" they kept talking about?

CHAPTER 2: CRACKS IN THE SYSTEM

A few weeks later, Lucy came back from grocery shopping, her face lined with frustration. She slapped the receipt on the kitchen counter with a sigh, showing me the numbers. Milk, eggs, bread—everything had shot up again.

"I don't know how they expect us to make it, Hank. How are we supposed to keep paying these prices?" she asked, her voice weary.

I wanted to say something comforting, but the words wouldn't come. I didn't know either. We were stretched thin as it was, and every month felt like a balancing act. I thought back to my dad, how he used to talk about politicians who stood up for the little guy. But where were those people now?

That night, after Lucy went to bed, I couldn't shake the feeling that we were being left out of the picture. I sat down at the computer, something I rarely did, and started reading. I wanted to understand why things felt so broken, to figure out if there was some hidden reason behind the way our lives were changing. At first, I just searched for articles on the economy, but it was the same old story—analysts talking in circles, charts showing that things were improving, stats on job growth. None of it matched the reality I was living.

Then I stumbled across a blog that caught my eye. It was written by a man who called himself a "political outsider," and he was talking about something I hadn't considered before—the connection between big corporations and politics, how they fed off each other. According to him, politicians on both sides were in bed with big money, working together to keep regular folks like me exactly where we were: just comfortable enough to keep working, but always struggling.

The more I read, the more something inside me stirred. I'd never thought much about corporations or who funded politicians before, but this guy laid it out in a way that made sense. He pointed out how, year after year, people in office made decisions that seemed to benefit the wealthy while leaving the rest of us to pick up the scraps. It was like they were building a system designed to keep us locked in place, while they profited.

I felt a mixture of anger and shame. Anger that this might be true, and shame that I hadn't noticed it sooner. I thought of all the times I'd shrugged off claims of corruption or brushed aside talk of "rigged" systems. But now, I wasn't so sure. Maybe I'd been too quick to dismiss it all. I kept reading, kept digging, and by the time I finally crawled into bed, my mind was racing with thoughts I couldn't shake.

Over the next few weeks, I started looking at the world through a different lens. It was like putting on a new pair of glasses—suddenly, everything seemed clearer, and not in a good way. I watched the news with a skeptical eye, seeing past the polished words and carefully crafted messages. Every time a politician spoke about "progress" or "growth," I couldn't help but feel like they were talking to someone else, not people like me.

One evening, I brought it up to a couple of the guys at work. I mentioned how things seemed to be set up to keep us just barely afloat, while the folks in charge lined their pockets. A few of them shrugged, like they'd heard it all before, but Jim—an older guy who'd been around since before I started—looked at me, his face grim.

"Funny you say that, Hank. It's been like this for a while, but most folks just accept it, think that's how things have to be," he said, scratching his chin. "But maybe they don't."

Hearing Jim agree gave me a strange sense of relief. I'd been feeling like a stranger in my own skin, questioning things I'd always taken for granted, and knowing that others felt the same way helped me feel less alone. It was like a silent awakening, a slow realization that, just maybe, there was more to this whole thing than I'd ever been willing to see.

And so, without even realizing it, I started paying attention in a way I never had before, questioning the narratives I'd always accepted. It was uncomfortable, like unlearning something I'd been taught all my life. But once I'd started, I couldn't stop. It felt like opening a door I couldn't close, and part of me didn't want to. I was drawn in, wanting to understand, to see where it led.

CHAPTER 3: A STEP DOWN THE RABBIT HOLE

It was just a few days after that conversation with Lucy when I found myself sitting in front of the computer again, scrolling through articles and videos with titles like "The Truth About Corporate Control" and "The Secrets Behind the Media." I knew I was diving into something different from the usual evening news, but I couldn't seem to stop myself. The more I watched, the more I read, the more I felt like I'd been walking around with blinders on my whole life.

One night, I stumbled onto a podcast called "Voices of Freedom." The host was a former journalist who'd left mainstream media because, he claimed, he'd grown tired of telling half-truths. He spoke calmly, laying out his thoughts with a kind of ease that was unsettling. He talked about how the major news networks all fed us the same stories, almost word-for-word, and how those stories were often curated to serve people in power. It was nothing flashy, nothing you'd see plastered across a headline, but his words had a kind of weight to them.

He called it the "corporate-political complex"—a network of powerful companies and politicians working together, doing everything they could to stay in control. According to him, they didn't want us asking questions. They wanted us quiet and compliant, content with whatever information they fed us.

I sat there, leaning forward, nodding along without even

realizing it. He talked about how the corporations that owned the media were the same ones donating millions to political campaigns, ensuring that no matter which party was in charge, the rules stayed the same for them. It all felt like a game, one they were rigging to keep folks like me on the sidelines.

As I listened, I remembered all the years I'd watched the news, trusting that they were giving it to me straight. I thought about the politicians I'd voted for, the rallies and speeches I'd watched, believing that they were on my side. But now, it was as if the veil had been lifted. Maybe I was just a pawn to them, another number, another vote. It was a bitter thought, and I couldn't shake it.

After a while, I turned off the computer, but I sat there in the dark for a long time, just thinking. I felt like I'd been living in a fog, like there was this whole hidden layer to the world that I was only now beginning to see. And I wasn't sure if I wanted to know more, but I couldn't deny that part of me was curious.

The next day, I mentioned a bit of it to Joe at work, testing the waters. We were on a break, sitting on the edge of a concrete step outside the building, watching the afternoon light fade.

"You ever feel like they're all in it together?" I asked, trying to keep my voice casual.

Joe took a drag from his cigarette, exhaling slowly. "You mean the politicians?"

"Yeah. It's like… I don't know, like they're all just playing their parts, saying what we want to hear. But when you look at what they actually do, it's like nothing really changes for us, you know?"

Joe looked at me, his gaze thoughtful. "Hank, that's just the way it is. Always has been. They don't care about us. They're too busy getting fat on their donor money and fancy perks."

I nodded, but his answer only stirred up more questions. If that was just "how it is," why hadn't I seen it before? Had I been blind, too caught up in my own life to notice what was happening right in front of me? The thought gnawed at me, lingering long after our conversation ended.

CHAPTER 4: GETTING DRAWN IN

As the weeks went on, I kept returning to that podcast, diving deeper into articles and videos, following thread after thread of information that seemed to lead further away from what I'd always known. It became almost like a habit. I'd finish my dinner, wait until Lucy went off to bed, and then I'd pull up my laptop and start searching, reading, listening. It was a quiet obsession, something I couldn't explain, even to myself.

One night, I found a video titled "The Media Machine," which claimed that nearly all the news we see is controlled by a small handful of companies. They listed off names—big ones, recognizable names that owned dozens of networks, websites, and newspapers. The video laid out how these companies were all connected, how they each had close ties to politicians and lobbyists. As I watched, I felt a chill settle over me. It was like I was seeing the media for the first time, not as an unbiased source, but as a tool used to keep us in line.

The next morning, I mentioned it to Lucy while we were having coffee. I hadn't planned on bringing it up, but the words slipped out before I could stop them.

"You ever wonder if maybe the news doesn't tell us the whole truth?" I asked, trying to keep my tone casual.

Lucy looked up from her cup, giving me a curious look. "What do you mean?"

"Like... I don't know, maybe they only show us the stories they want us to see. Maybe they're all connected to the same big corporations, the same powerful people. It's like they're just telling us what they want us to believe."

Lucy's face softened, and she reached across the table to pat my hand. "Hank, you're starting to sound like one of those conspiracy theorists," she said with a gentle laugh. "I know things aren't perfect, but do you really think the news is trying to control us?"

I shrugged, feeling a bit sheepish under her gaze. "I don't know, Lucy. But sometimes it feels like they're all reading from the same script, like they're not telling us everything."

She just smiled, shaking her head. "Hank, there's so much information out there. Not everything is some grand conspiracy. Sometimes, things are just what they seem."

I wanted to believe her. But deep down, I felt like I was seeing something real, something she couldn't understand. It wasn't that I thought everything was a conspiracy, but it was hard to ignore the patterns, the way the news seemed to echo the same talking points, no matter the network.

CHAPTER 5: RECONSIDERING THE ELECTION

The idea of the media as a tool kept circling in my mind, and before long, I found myself thinking back to the 2016 election. Back then, I'd dismissed Trump's talk of a "rigged" system as nothing more than hot air, a way to stir up his base. But now, with what I'd learned about corporate control and media bias, I started wondering if maybe I'd been too quick to judge.

One evening, after everyone had gone to bed, I decided to revisit some of Trump's old speeches. I found clips of him from his rallies, talking about corruption, about "draining the swamp," about how Washington was full of career politicians who only cared about themselves. He talked about the "deep state," a term I'd heard back then but never really thought much about. But now, with all the pieces I'd been putting together, his words took on a different meaning.

I watched him talk about how the political system was rigged, how the people in power only cared about their own interests. It was strange, hearing those words again after all these years. Part of me still felt skeptical, like he was just playing to the crowd. But another part of me couldn't shake the feeling that he was onto something.

The more I watched, the more I started to see Trump in a different light. He wasn't perfect, that much was clear. But he was saying things that no other politician had said, things that resonated with the doubts I'd been feeling. I didn't know if I believed his claim that the election was "stolen," but I couldn't deny that he was speaking to a truth I'd only recently started to understand.

The next day, I brought it up to Joe again. We were working side-by-side, welding a new frame for a project, the sparks dancing in the air around us.

"You remember back in 2016, when Trump kept saying the system was rigged?" I asked, trying to keep my tone casual.

Joe looked at me, his face a mixture of curiosity and caution. "Yeah, I remember. Why?"

"Well, I was just thinking... maybe he wasn't wrong. Maybe there really is something to that. I mean, look at how things have turned out. Doesn't it seem like the people in power are just looking out for themselves?"

Joe nodded slowly, his expression thoughtful. "I suppose there's some truth to that. But it's hard to know what's real and what's just talk, you know?"

"Yeah," I said, feeling a strange sense of relief. "I just... I don't know. It's hard to ignore, that's all."

As I spoke, I felt a weight lift off my shoulders. I still didn't know what to believe, but at least I wasn't alone in feeling this way. And that, somehow, made the uncertainty a little easier to bear.

CHAPTER 6: THE WEB GROWS

The deeper I went into my research, the more I felt like I was uncovering a hidden world, a web of connections and secrets that stretched far beyond what I'd ever imagined. I found forums where people shared their own discoveries, stories about how they'd come to see the world in a new light. They talked about politicians, corporations, media moguls—all part of a system designed to keep the average person in the dark.

One of the most compelling things I found was a documentary about the "deep state." The filmmaker claimed that there was a network of people behind the scenes—unelected officials, bureaucrats, intelligence officers—who held real power, no matter who was in office. According to him, these people didn't answer to the public. They worked quietly, behind closed doors, shaping policies and decisions in ways that benefited themselves and their allies.

I watched, transfixed, as the documentary laid out example after example of how this "deep state" influenced everything from foreign policy to domestic issues. It was like seeing the world through a new lens, one that made sense of all the frustrations I'd been feeling. It explained why things never seemed to change, why every election brought more of the same, regardless of who won.

That night, I tried to explain it to Lucy, hoping she'd understand. I told her about the connections I'd found, the way the media and government seemed to be part of the same machine. She listened, her face thoughtful, but I could see the doubt in her eyes.

"Hank, I know you're worried, but this sounds… well, it sounds like a lot," she said gently. "Do you really think there's a group of people secretly running everything?"

"I don't know, Lucy," I said, my voice barely above a whisper. "But it makes sense, doesn't it? Think about it. Look at how things are, how nothing ever seems to change."

She nodded, but I could tell she wasn't convinced. And that was fine, I supposed. I didn't expect her to see things the way I did. But deep down, I knew I couldn't ignore what I'd found. Whether or not Lucy believed me, I felt like I was finally starting to see the world for what it was.

CHAPTER 7:
LOSING TOUCH

The deeper I went down this path, the more I felt like my world was splitting in two. By day, I was still Hank, the welder who showed up to work, put in his hours, and went home to his wife. But by night, when I sat alone in front of my computer, digging into forums, watching videos, reading articles that fed my growing doubts, I was someone else—someone with questions, with convictions, with a gnawing need to know the truth.

But with every late night, every quiet hour spent piecing together what I thought was a clearer picture of the world, I felt myself drifting further from the life I'd always known. The conversations I'd once had with friends, family, and even Lucy seemed shallow, out of touch. The things we used to talk about—work, our town, the little things in life—now felt like distractions from the bigger truths I was learning. It was as if I was walking through the world in a fog, seeing things differently from everyone around me.

One evening, I brought up some of my thoughts to Lucy again. She was sitting on the couch, flipping through a magazine, and I was scrolling through an article that talked about the ties between politicians and media networks.

"Lucy," I said, looking up, "did you know that nearly all the major news networks are owned by just a handful of companies? And those companies have connections to politicians on both sides. It's like… it's like they're all working together."

She looked up from her magazine, her expression patient but

wary. "Hank, you've mentioned this before," she said gently. "But does it really matter? I mean, what can we do about it? Maybe it's better not to dwell on things we can't change."

Her words stung more than I wanted to admit. I knew she was just trying to keep the peace, to bring things back to normal. But I couldn't just "not dwell" on it. I'd seen too much, learned too much to ignore it now. The truth was out there, and I wasn't willing to turn a blind eye.

"Maybe," I said, trying to keep my tone calm. "But don't you think it's important to know what's really happening? I mean, this isn't just some conspiracy theory. It's out there for anyone to see if they look hard enough."

Lucy sighed, closing her magazine and placing it on the coffee table. "Hank, I just… I worry about you," she said, her voice barely above a whisper. "You're always reading these things, getting worked up. It's like you're drifting away from everything we've built. I miss the days when we'd talk about other things."

Her words hung in the air, filling the room with a heavy silence. I felt a pang of guilt, realizing how much my focus had shifted over the past few months. But at the same time, I couldn't shake the feeling that she didn't understand, that she couldn't understand what it felt like to see the world with new eyes.

"I know, Lucy," I said finally, my voice soft. "But I can't just pretend everything's fine. I feel like… like there's so much at stake. Don't you want to know the truth?"

She looked away, her expression a mixture of sadness and frustration. "Maybe. But not if it means losing you."

That night, as I lay beside her in bed, I couldn't shake the feeling that something was slipping away. I was still here, still the same man she'd married, but in a way, I was already somewhere else— somewhere she couldn't reach. And as much as I wanted to bridge that gap, to bring her along with me, I didn't know how. The path I was on felt too important, too real to turn back from, even if it meant losing the connection we once had.

CHAPTER 8: THE ECHO CHAMBER

After that conversation with Lucy, I found myself turning even more to the online communities I'd joined. These forums, these threads—they were the only places where I felt truly understood. There, I could talk openly, share my thoughts, ask questions without fear of judgment. It was a relief, like finding a place where I could finally let down my guard.

I started following a few regulars on the forum. One of them, a guy who went by the username "Patriot47," posted frequently, sharing links to articles and videos that challenged mainstream narratives. He seemed like he knew what he was talking about, like he'd been down this road before. I found myself drawn to his posts, reading every word, taking notes on his recommendations. Through his posts, I found more information, more sources that aligned with my growing beliefs.

Patriot47 wasn't just knowledgeable; he was passionate. He talked about "awakening the masses," about fighting for truth and freedom. He wrote about how they—whoever "they" were—wanted to keep us silent, compliant, lost in our own little bubbles while they pulled the strings. His words resonated with me, each one feeling like a call to action.

Before long, I found myself engaging with him directly. I'd comment on his posts, ask questions, share my own thoughts. He'd respond quickly, always encouraging, always urging me to dig deeper, to question more. We weren't just strangers on a forum —we were allies in a shared mission, soldiers in a battle for truth.

But as I spent more time in these spaces, I started to notice a shift in myself. My patience with people outside the group, people who didn't see what I saw, was wearing thin. Conversations with friends, even casual chats at work, began to feel hollow, meaningless. I found myself growing irritated with anyone who didn't share my beliefs, who dismissed my questions or tried to steer the conversation back to "normal" topics.

At first, I thought it was just frustration—a natural reaction to feeling misunderstood. But over time, I realized it was more than that. It was as if I'd entered an echo chamber, a place where only my beliefs were validated, where dissenting voices were silenced or ridiculed. In the forum, there was an unspoken rule: if you weren't with us, you were against us. And the more I engaged, the more that mindset seeped into my own way of thinking.

I tried to brush it off, telling myself that I was simply committed, passionate about the truth. But there was a small voice in the back of my mind, a whisper of doubt that I couldn't quite ignore. Was I really seeing the world clearly? Or was I just surrounding myself with people who thought like me, shutting out anyone who dared to question?

The thought lingered, a faint shadow in the back of my mind. But I pushed it aside, telling myself that the truth was worth any price, that I was on the right path, even if it meant losing touch with those who couldn't—or wouldn't—see what I saw.

CHAPTER 9: A RIFT WITH LUCY

The tension between me and Lucy had been simmering for weeks, a quiet but persistent presence that hung over our home like a dark cloud. We still talked, still went through the motions of daily life, but it was as if there was a wall between us, a barrier I didn't know how to break down.

One evening, after dinner, I sat on the couch, scrolling through my laptop, reading an article about election fraud—another topic that had recently caught my attention. I was engrossed, absorbed in the words, when Lucy sat down beside me, her face etched with worry.

"Hank, we need to talk," she said, her voice soft but serious.

I looked up, sensing the weight of her words. "Sure, what's on your mind?"

She took a deep breath, her hands clasped tightly in her lap. "I feel like... like I'm losing you, Hank," she said, her voice barely above a whisper. "You're always so wrapped up in these theories, these forums. It's like you're here, but you're not really here. I miss the man I married."

Her words hit me like a punch to the gut. I could see the pain in her eyes, the fear that had been building up inside her for weeks. I wanted to tell her that she was wrong, that I was still the same man, but I knew that wasn't true. I had changed. I'd seen things, learned things that I couldn't unsee, and there was no going back.

"I'm sorry, Lucy," I said, reaching for her hand. "I know it's been a lot. But... don't you understand? I feel like I've been lied to my whole life, and now I'm finally starting to see the truth. I just need to know what's really going on."

She shook her head, tears glistening in her eyes. "Hank, I don't want to spend my life living in fear and suspicion. I don't want to lose you to a world of shadows and secrets. Can't we just... go back to the way things were?"

Her words tugged at something deep inside me, a longing for the simplicity of the life we'd once shared. But that life felt like a distant memory, a place I could never return to. I'd come too far, seen too much to just turn back.

"I wish I could, Lucy," I said, my voice breaking. "But I can't ignore what I've found. I'm sorry."

She nodded, her eyes welling up with tears. "I know this is what you really believe, Hank. I just wish you wouldn't let it take over your whole life like this."

That night, as she lay beside me in bed, I felt the weight of her words pressing down on me. I was still here, still the same man in many ways, but I knew, deep down, that I was already drifting away. The truth I'd been searching for had come at a cost, and I wasn't sure if it was a price I was willing to pay.

CHAPTER 10: THE AWAKENING

The decision to attend my first local meeting felt monumental. I'd spent so many hours in front of my computer, wrapped up in the world of forums and podcasts, surrounded by voices but never faces. For months, I'd been gathering fragments of information, trying to piece together a picture of the world that made sense to me. Now, I was ready to step out from behind the screen, to take a real step into this new reality.

The meeting was scheduled for a Saturday afternoon, in a modest community center on the edge of town. I'd driven by the place a hundred times but never given it much thought. It was one of those plain, nondescript buildings that could just as easily be a bingo hall as a church meeting room. As I walked in, the first thing that struck me was how ordinary it all felt. Folding chairs were set up in a circle, and people were gathered in small groups, chatting quietly, sipping coffee from styrofoam cups.

A man with a thick salt-and-pepper mustache came over to me, extending his hand. "Hey there. You must be Hank," he said, his grip firm but friendly. "I'm Bill. Glad you could make it."

"Thanks, Bill," I replied, feeling a mixture of nerves and relief. Here I was, finally, face-to-face with people who might understand what I'd been going through.

Bill gestured toward the chairs, and we joined the others. As I settled in, I took a moment to look around. There were about fifteen of us, ranging from a woman who looked like she was in her late twenties, wearing a "Don't Tread on Me" T-shirt, to an elderly man with a weathered face and calloused hands, sitting quietly with his arms crossed.

Bill cleared his throat, bringing the room to attention. "All right, everyone, let's get started. First off, I want to welcome Hank. He's new here, but I think he's going to fit in just fine."

The group turned to me, nodding and smiling in encouragement. I managed a small smile in return, still feeling out of place but beginning to relax.

"Why don't we start by introducing ourselves?" Bill suggested, and we went around the circle. Each person shared a bit about themselves, how they'd come to be here, and what had drawn them to this gathering. The stories were a lot like mine—people feeling disillusioned, like the world they'd trusted had somehow turned against them. Some had been coming to these meetings for years; others, like me, were here for the first time, searching for answers.

One woman, Linda, spoke about her concerns over rising taxes and government overreach. She worked as a nurse and felt like she was drowning under the weight of new regulations that, in her words, "cared more about checking boxes than actually helping people." She looked at me as she spoke, her face a mixture of frustration and determination.

Then there was Marcus, a mechanic with grease-stained hands and a deep, gravelly voice. He talked about how he'd been feeling like an outsider in his own country, like his values didn't matter anymore. "It's like they're trying to push us out," he said, shaking his head. "All this talk about change, about progress... but at what cost? They don't care about us. They never did."

As I listened, I felt a growing sense of solidarity. These people understood my frustrations. They saw the same issues, the same cracks in the system that I'd been seeing. The feeling was a powerful one, like I'd finally found a place where I belonged.

When it was my turn, I hesitated, unsure of where to begin. "I... I guess I've just been feeling like something's off," I said, struggling to put months of confusion and doubt into words. "I used to trust what I saw on the news, what I heard from politicians. But lately...

I don't know. It's like everything is designed to keep us in the dark."

There were nods around the room, quiet murmurs of agreement. Encouraged, I continued. "I've been reading, watching videos, trying to understand. And the more I learn, the more it feels like the people in power aren't telling us the whole truth. Like they're keeping us in the dark on purpose."

"Exactly," Marcus said, leaning forward. "That's how they keep us in line. By feeding us just enough information to make us feel informed but never enough to see the whole picture."

The energy in the room was electric. People nodded, spoke in agreement, and shared their own thoughts and theories. I felt like I was finally speaking openly, saying things I'd held back for fear of being dismissed or called paranoid. But here, I wasn't just another voice in the crowd. I was part of something.

Bill started talking about their goals as a group. They wanted to "wake people up," to help others see the truth about the world we lived in. He mentioned local projects they were working on, like organizing town hall meetings to discuss government policies and writing letters to local representatives about issues they felt were ignored by the mainstream.

"We may not have the resources those folks at the top do, but we've got something they don't—passion and numbers," Bill said, his eyes bright with conviction. "If we stand together, if we make our voices heard, they can't ignore us forever."

I nodded, feeling a swell of pride. I'd spent so long feeling isolated, like my doubts were something to be ashamed of. But here, those doubts were strengths. These people didn't see me as paranoid or misguided. They saw me as someone who wanted answers, someone who was willing to look beyond the surface and question what he'd been told.

After a while, the group broke off into smaller discussions. Linda came over and introduced herself more formally, asking about my background, what had led me here. I told her about the frustration I'd been feeling, the late nights spent reading and searching, trying to make sense of everything.

"I know exactly what you mean," she said, nodding. "It's like waking up from a dream, isn't it? One day, you realize that all those things you took for granted were just illusions. And once you see it, there's no going back."

We talked for a while, swapping stories about the moments that had made us question what we'd always believed. She told me about her family, how she'd tried to talk to them about the things she'd learned, only to be met with skepticism and disbelief.

"It's hard, isn't it?" she said, her voice soft. "Losing people because they can't understand. They think I'm crazy, like I'm seeing things that aren't there. But it's all there, plain as day. They just don't want to see it."

I nodded, understanding exactly what she meant. I thought about Lucy, about the tension that had been building between us, the way she looked at me with a mixture of concern and frustration whenever I talked about my beliefs. I wondered if she'd ever truly understand, or if this was something I'd have to face alone.

As the evening wore on, the group came back together for a final discussion. Bill talked about upcoming events, ways we could get involved in the community, and make our voices heard. He emphasized the importance of unity, of standing together even when others tried to tear us down.

"Look, they want us to feel isolated," he said, his voice calm but firm. "They want us to believe that we're alone, that we're just a bunch of fringe thinkers with no power. But that's a lie. There are more of us than they want us to believe. And as long as we stick together, as long as we keep pushing, they can't silence us."

I left that night feeling more invigorated than I had in months. I'd finally found a community that understood me, people who saw the world the way I did. For the first time in a long time, I felt like I wasn't alone. I was part of something bigger, something that mattered.

On the drive home, I replayed the night's conversations in my mind, feeling a sense of purpose I hadn't felt before. I knew there would be challenges ahead, that not everyone in my life would understand the path I'd chosen. But I didn't care. I was awake now, and there was no going back. The truth was out there, and I was ready to find it—no matter the cost.

CHAPTER 11: THE LOCAL MEETING GROUP

After that first meeting, it was like a new world had opened up for me. I went to bed that night feeling more alive, more connected, and more understood than I had in months. Finally, I was surrounded by people who didn't just nod politely or listen out of obligation—they genuinely cared about the same things I did. And they were willing to talk about it, to dive into the uncomfortable truths that had been gnawing at me for so long.

The next week, I attended another meeting, eager to see those familiar faces and hear more of the conversations that had started to feel like lifelines. This time, I recognized people by name—Bill, Linda, Marcus, and a few others. We exchanged nods and smiles as we settled into our seats, and I felt that same sense of camaraderie and purpose filling the room. We weren't just a group of strangers. We were allies, bound together by our search for truth.

As we began, Bill stood up and announced that we'd be organizing a "community outreach" event. The plan was to set up a booth at the town's upcoming farmers' market, where we could talk to people about the issues we felt were being ignored by the mainstream media. There was a quiet murmur of excitement in the room—this was our chance to reach out, to share our perspectives with people who might feel just as confused, just as disillusioned as we once had.

"I know not everyone is comfortable with public speaking," Bill said, looking around the room with a gentle smile. "But this isn't about arguing or convincing people we're right. It's about planting seeds. Just letting people know that they're not alone, that there are others out there who see things differently."

I felt a thrill of nervous energy. The idea of standing at a booth, talking to strangers about what I'd learned, was intimidating. But at the same time, it felt like the right thing to do. I'd spent months reading, questioning, digging for answers. Now, it was my turn to share what I'd found, to help others open their eyes.

Linda raised her hand, volunteering to help organize the materials for the booth. Marcus said he'd bring some flyers he'd printed with information about media bias, government overreach, and corporate control. People around the room nodded, offering their support, their encouragement. I found myself nodding along, feeling a part of something bigger, something that mattered.

Bill turned to me with a smile. "Hank, would you be willing to help us out? I know you're new here, but sometimes a fresh perspective is just what we need."

I hesitated, glancing around the room, but the encouraging smiles and nods gave me the confidence I needed. "Sure, I'd be glad to," I said, feeling a surge of pride. I wasn't just a spectator anymore. I was an active part of this movement, someone willing to stand up and speak out.

We spent the rest of the meeting going over details—who would bring what, where we'd set up, what kind of questions we might expect. By the time we wrapped up, I felt a sense of purpose that was almost overwhelming. For the first time in a long time, I was doing something that mattered, something that could make a difference.

As we all filed out of the building, Marcus clapped a hand on my shoulder. "Good to have you on board, Hank. We need more people like you—folks who aren't afraid to ask questions."

"Thanks, Marcus," I said, feeling a warmth in my chest. "I'm glad to be here. It feels… it feels right."

He nodded, his expression serious. "We're lucky to have you,

Hank. Remember, this isn't just about one meeting or one event. This is about changing minds, opening eyes. It's about making sure the people in power know we're not just going to sit back and take whatever they throw at us."

I nodded, feeling the weight of his words. This wasn't just about curiosity anymore. It was about justice, about truth, about standing up for what was right.

CHAPTER 12: FACING DOUBTS AND CHALLENGES

In the days leading up to the event, I couldn't stop thinking about what we were doing. I'd spent years feeling like just another cog in the machine, going through the motions, working, paying bills, and never asking too many questions. But now, things were different. I felt like I was part of a movement, a real cause. And as empowering as that felt, there was a part of me that couldn't shake a lingering doubt.

One evening, as I sat on the couch reviewing some of the flyers Marcus had given me, Lucy sat down beside me. She glanced at the stack of papers in my hand, her brow furrowing with concern.

"Hank, what's all this?" she asked, her tone hesitant.

I took a deep breath, knowing this conversation was coming. "It's for the outreach event we're doing at the farmers' market. We're setting up a booth, handing out information about media control, government overreach... that kind of thing."

Lucy looked down, her expression troubled. "I don't know, Hank. This... it all seems a little intense. Are you sure you want to get involved in something like this?"

I nodded, feeling a surge of defensiveness. "Lucy, I've spent months looking into this stuff. I know it's hard to understand, but people deserve to know the truth. They deserve to know that the media and the government aren't always working in our best interest."

She sighed, reaching out to take my hand. "I understand that you're passionate about this, Hank. But... it just seems like it's taking over your life. Every conversation, every spare moment—it's all about this. I miss the days when we'd talk about other things, when we'd just... be together."

Her words hurt, but I tried to keep my tone calm. "Lucy, this isn't just some hobby. It's about making a difference, about standing up for what's right. Don't you see that?"

She looked down, her hand slipping away from mine. "I do, Hank. But I also see what it's doing to you, to us. Just... be careful, okay? I don't want to lose you to all of this."

The conversation left a sour taste in my mouth, a lingering sense of guilt that I tried to push away. I knew she was worried, but I couldn't let her doubts hold me back. I'd come too far, learned too much. I was finally part of something real, something that mattered. And I wasn't about to turn back now.

CHAPTER 13: THE OUTREACH EVENT

The morning of the farmers' market was bright and clear, with a crispness in the air that signaled the arrival of fall. I arrived early, helping Marcus and Linda set up our booth. We arranged flyers, pamphlets, and posters that outlined our main points—media bias, government overreach, corporate control. It was all neatly laid out, designed to catch the eye and spark curiosity.

As the market began to fill up with shoppers, families, and vendors, I felt a mix of excitement and nerves. This was our chance to reach people, to share what we'd learned. But at the same time, I worried about how they'd react. Would they listen? Would they dismiss us as conspiracy theorists?

The first hour was slow. People glanced at our booth, some taking a flyer, others giving us a wary look before moving on. I could see the skepticism in their eyes, the way they seemed to question what we were doing. But then, something shifted.

A man in his forties approached, looking at our posters with interest. "What's all this about?" he asked, picking up one of our pamphlets.

I stepped forward, feeling a surge of confidence. "It's about media control and how the corporations that own the news networks are connected to the government," I explained. "A lot of people don't realize how controlled our information is. We're just here to share what we've found."

He nodded, flipping through the pamphlet. "I've been thinking the same thing, actually. It's like every channel says the same thing, almost word-for-word."

"That's exactly right," Marcus chimed in, stepping up beside me. "They're all following the same script. They want us to believe we're getting the full story, but in reality, they're just giving us the version that benefits them."

As we talked, a small crowd began to gather around us. People asked questions, shared their own frustrations, nodded in agreement. Some were skeptical, but others seemed genuinely curious, willing to listen. I felt a rush of pride, a sense of purpose that was almost overwhelming. This was what we were here for—to plant seeds, to make people question, to help them see the truth.

Throughout the day, we spoke with dozens of people, some more receptive than others. I could see the glimmer of recognition in their eyes, the way they'd nod thoughtfully, as if a piece of the puzzle had finally clicked into place. And for each person who walked away with a pamphlet or a flyer, I felt a sense of accomplishment. We were making a difference, one conversation at a time.

As the day drew to a close, Bill gathered us around, his face beaming with pride. "We did good work today, folks," he said, clapping Marcus on the back. "We're not going to change the world overnight, but today... today, we made a start."

I nodded, feeling a swell of pride. For so long, I'd felt powerless, like my voice didn't matter. But now, I was part of something bigger, something that could make a real impact. As we packed up the booth, I couldn't shake the feeling that this was just the beginning—that there was so much more work to be done, so many more people to reach.

On the drive home, I thought about all the conversations we'd had, all the people who'd stopped to listen. I felt a sense of satisfaction, a deep, unshakable certainty that I was on the right path. I was no longer just a man searching for answers—I was a man with a purpose, a mission. And I was ready to do whatever it took to see it through.

CHAPTER 14: A GROWING DIVIDE

In the days following the farmers' market, I couldn't stop thinking about the event. Every conversation, every curious face, every pamphlet that found its way into someone's hands—these moments stuck with me like snapshots, small but powerful reminders that we were making a difference. For the first time in my life, I felt like my voice mattered, like I was part of something that could genuinely change people's lives.

But as invigorating as the experience had been, it also highlighted just how much I was drifting from the life I once knew. The people I'd met at the meeting, the community we were building—they understood me, validated my thoughts, encouraged my questions. They saw the world the way I did, and that gave me a deep sense of purpose. But outside of those meetings, I felt increasingly isolated, like I was living in a different reality from everyone else.

Lucy and I hadn't really spoken about the farmers' market, and part of me was relieved. I knew she was skeptical, and I didn't want to face another conversation where she questioned my choices. But her silence left a void, a sense of distance that only seemed to grow as the days passed.

One evening, as I was washing up after dinner, Lucy finally brought it up. "So… how was the farmers' market?" she asked, her tone neutral, but her eyes wary.

"It was great," I said, trying to keep my voice casual. "We had a lot of good conversations, handed out a bunch of flyers. I think we really got through to some people."

She nodded, but I could tell from her expression that she wasn't convinced. "I'm glad it went well," she said, her tone careful. "But Hank… do you ever worry that maybe you're getting too deep into all of this?"

For a moment, I didn't know how to respond. Part of me wanted to brush it off, to reassure her that everything was fine. But another part of me felt a surge of defensiveness. She didn't understand. She hadn't seen what I'd seen, hadn't felt that gnawing need to know the truth.

"Too deep?" I asked, my voice sharper than I intended. "Lucy, it's about making a difference, about standing up for what's right. Don't you see that?"

She looked down, her expression a mixture of sadness and frustration. "I know you believe that, Hank. But it feels like… like I'm losing you. You're so focused on these issues, these theories. It's like there's no room left for anything else."

I reflected on this, but I couldn't shake the feeling that she was missing the point. This wasn't just about curiosity or passion—it was about justice, about truth.

"Lucy, I know this is hard for you to understand," I said, trying to keep my voice steady. "But I can't ignore what I've found. This is important—more important than anything else right now."

She nodded, a tear slipping down her cheek. "I just hope you know what you're doing, Hank. I hope you don't lose yourself in all of this."

That night, as I lay beside her in bed, her words echoed in my mind. I was still here, still Hank. But in a way, I was already somewhere else, somewhere she couldn't follow.

CHAPTER 15: DEEPER CONNECTIONS

After the success of the farmers' market, Bill suggested that we take our outreach a step further. He wanted us to hold regular meetings, open to anyone in the community who was interested in learning more about the issues we were passionate about. The idea was simple: create a space where people could come, ask questions, and learn the truth about the world around them.

The first meeting was held in a small room at the local library, with folding chairs arranged in a circle and a few posters on the walls outlining our main points. It was modest, but it felt right. This was a place where people could come together, where they could voice their concerns, their doubts, their questions without fear of judgment.

As people trickled in, I felt a familiar surge of excitement. These weren't just strangers—they were potential allies, people who, like me, were searching for answers. I recognized some faces from the farmers' market, and a few others I'd seen around town. They looked curious, eager, maybe even a little apprehensive. But there was a shared sense of purpose, a feeling that we were all here for the same reason.

Bill started things off with a brief introduction, explaining our mission, our goals, our commitment to uncovering the truth. He spoke with a calm conviction that was both reassuring and inspiring, his words resonating with everyone in the room.

"We're not here to tell you what to think," he said, his gaze steady. "We're here to encourage you to question, to look beyond the surface. The world is a complex place, and there are forces at work that don't always have our best interests at heart. Our job is to ask questions, to seek out the truth, even if it's uncomfortable."

As he spoke, I felt a sense of pride and belonging that was almost overwhelming. This wasn't just a group of curious minds. This was a movement, a mission, a community of people who were willing to stand up and fight for the truth.

After Bill's introduction, we opened the floor to questions. People raised their hands, voiced their concerns, shared their own experiences. Some talked about their frustration with the media, their doubts about the government. Others spoke about feeling isolated, like they were the only ones who saw the cracks in the system. It was a safe space, a place where we could all be honest, vulnerable, real.

When it was my turn to speak, I shared my story—how I'd started questioning things, how I'd found the forum, how the meetings had changed my life. I talked about the feeling of isolation, of being dismissed, of losing touch with the people I loved. And as I spoke, I saw nods of understanding, faces that mirrored my own journey.

Linda spoke next, sharing her frustration with the health care system and how it had pushed her into questioning other areas of life. Marcus talked about the struggles he faced as a small business owner, how the government regulations seemed designed to crush people like him. Each story was unique, but they all shared a common thread—a sense of betrayal, of disillusionment, of wanting something better.

By the end of the meeting, I felt a renewed sense of purpose. This wasn't just about me, or about any one of us. It was about all of us, about building a community of people who were willing to question, to challenge, to fight for the truth. We weren't just individuals anymore. We were a movement, a force to be reckoned with.

As we packed up, Bill pulled me aside, his expression serious but proud. "You did good today, Hank," he said, clapping me on the shoulder. "We need people like you, people who aren't afraid to speak up."

"Thanks, Bill," I said, feeling a swell of pride. "I just… I want to make a difference. I want people to see what I've seen."

He nodded, his gaze intense. "And they will, Hank. Little by little, they will."

CHAPTER 16: STRAINED RELATIONSHIPS

As my involvement in the group deepened, so did the tension between me and the people around me. Lucy tried to be supportive, but I could see the worry in her eyes, the way she avoided bringing up certain topics, the way she looked at me with a mixture of sadness and fear. It was as if she was watching me drift away, powerless to bring me back.

One evening, we had friends over for dinner—an old couple we'd known for years, people who'd been part of our lives since we first moved into our house. Normally, our conversations were light, easy, filled with laughter and shared memories. But that night, something shifted.

The topic of the recent election came up, and I found myself unable to hold back. I started talking about the things I'd learned, the corruption, the media bias, the hidden agendas that shaped our world. I spoke with a conviction that surprised even me, my words spilling out in a torrent of frustration and passion.

Our friends exchanged glances, their expressions wary, uncomfortable. I could see the doubt in their eyes, the way they seemed to pull back, to distance themselves from the intensity of my beliefs. And as I spoke, I realized that I was losing them, that my words were pushing them away, creating a divide that couldn't easily be bridged.

After they left, Lucy looked at me, her face a mixture of sadness and disappointment. "Hank... what's happening to you?" she asked, her voice soft but steady.

"What do you mean?" I asked, feeling a surge of defensiveness.

"You're different. You're so... intense. It's like everything has become about this, about these theories. I feel like I'm losing you, Hank. I feel like you're slipping away."

I realized the weight behind what she was saying, and I didn't know how to respond. I wanted to reassure her, to tell her that everything was fine, that nothing had changed. We both knew the reality, however.

"I'm sorry, Lucy," I said, my voice barely above a whisper. "But I can't ignore the truth. I can't go back to the way things were."

She looked away, a tear slipping down her cheek. "What you are doing is tearing us apart!"

That night, as I lay in bed, I felt a sense of loss that was almost overwhelming. I was on a path that I believed in, a path that felt right, but it was a lonely one, a path that seemed to be taking me further and further from the life I'd once known.

And as I drifted off to sleep, I couldn't shake the feeling that I was standing on the edge of something vast and uncertain, a journey that had no clear destination, no way back. I was searching for truth, for justice, for a purpose. But at what cost?

CHAPTER 17: TAKING THE LEAD

After weeks of organizing, meeting, and sharing our stories, Bill approached me with a new idea. He wanted to expand our group, to take it beyond the local library and reach more people. He suggested that we start hosting community forums—open events where we could invite people to come, listen, and ask questions.

"Hank," he said one evening after our regular meeting had wrapped up, "I've been watching you, and I think you'd be perfect to help lead these events. You've got the conviction, the passion. People listen to you."

His words caught me off guard. Me? Leading a community forum? I was just a regular guy, a welder who'd stumbled into this world by accident. But at the same time, something in me stirred at the thought. This wasn't just about sharing my beliefs anymore —it was about guiding others, helping them see the things I'd seen, feel the way I felt.

"I don't know, Bill," I said, rubbing the back of my neck. "I'm no public speaker."

He smiled, clapping me on the shoulder. "You don't have to be. Just be yourself. Talk from the heart. That's what people respond to."

After a few moments of thought, I nodded. "All right. I'll give it a shot."

The next week, I found myself standing at the front of a modest auditorium in the back of a local community center, facing a crowd of about thirty people. Some faces were familiar from our group, but there were others—strangers, people I didn't know but who had come out to hear what we had to say. I felt a wave of nervousness wash over me, but Bill's words echoed in my mind: *Just be yourself. Talk from the heart.*

I took a deep breath, scanning the faces in the crowd. "Thank you all for coming tonight," I began, my voice steady but cautious. "I'm not a politician, or a professor, or anyone special. I'm just a regular guy who started asking questions. And I'm here tonight because I believe those questions matter, because I believe we all have the right to know the truth about what's going on in our country."

As I spoke, the nerves started to fade. The words came easier, flowing naturally, fueled by the passion that had been building inside me for months. I talked about the things I'd learned— the media control, the corporate influence, the way politicians seemed to care more about their donors than the people who put them in office. I talked about the feeling of isolation, of searching for answers in a world that didn't seem interested in giving them.

By the time I finished, the crowd was silent, listening intently. I could see a mixture of emotions on their faces—curiosity, anger, even a little fear. But above all, there was understanding. They knew what I was talking about because they'd felt it too.

When I opened the floor for questions, hands shot up around the room. People asked about everything from the influence of money in politics to the way the media covered certain stories while ignoring others. I answered as best as I could, drawing from the things I'd read, the discussions we'd had in our meetings. And as I spoke, I felt a growing sense of confidence. This wasn't just a passing interest anymore. It was a mission, a purpose.

After the forum ended, several people came up to me, thanking me for speaking out, for giving voice to the things they'd been feeling. One man, a retired teacher, shook my hand and said, "You're doing something important, Hank. Don't stop. People need to hear this."

I drove home that night with a sense of accomplishment, a feeling that I was finally doing something that mattered. For so long, I'd felt like a cog in the machine, just going through the motions. But now, I was making a difference, helping people see the world in a new way.

Lucy was waiting for me when I got home, and I told her about the forum, the people who'd come up to me, the impact I felt I was making. She smiled, but there was a sadness in her eyes, a quiet worry that lingered even as she congratulated me.

"I'm happy for you, Hank," she said, her voice soft. "I just... I hope you remember who you are through all of this."

Her words left me unsettled, a reminder that the path I was on wasn't as straightforward as it seemed. But as I lay in bed that night, I felt a sense of purpose that outweighed the doubts, a conviction that I was doing the right thing.

CHAPTER 18: COMMITMENT AND CONSEQUENCES

The following weeks were a whirlwind of meetings, forums, and discussions. Word spread quickly about our events, and each week, more people showed up. Some were curious, others were skeptical, but they all had one thing in common: a desire to know the truth. I became a regular speaker, leading discussions, answering questions, sharing my story. The more I spoke, the more confident I became. This wasn't just a hobby or an interest anymore—it was a calling, a responsibility.

But as my involvement grew, so did the strain on my personal life. Lucy tried to be supportive, but I could see the toll it was taking on her. Our conversations grew shorter, more tense. She stopped asking about the meetings, and I stopped sharing, sensing that it only pushed her further away. The divide between us had become a chasm, and I didn't know how to bridge it.

One evening, after a particularly heated forum where we'd discussed media bias, I came home to find Lucy sitting on the couch, waiting for me. Her face was pale, her hands clenched tightly in her lap.

"Hank, we need to talk," she said, her voice barely above a whisper.

I sat down beside her, bracing myself for what was coming.

She took a deep breath, her gaze fixed on her hands. "Every time I look at you, it's like you're somewhere else. You're so wrapped up in these theories, these meetings. I don't even recognize you anymore."

"Lucy, I'm sorry," I said, my voice breaking. "But this... this is important to me. I feel like I'm finally doing something that matters."

She looked away, her shoulders slumping. "I just wish you could see what it's doing to us, Hank. I feel like I'm losing you, and I don't know how to bring you back."

We sat in silence, the weight of her words pressing down on me. I wanted to comfort her, to reassure her that everything would be okay. But deep down, I knew that my path had taken me somewhere she couldn't follow.

That night, I lay in bed, staring at the ceiling, feeling a mixture of pride and regret. I was doing something important, something that felt right. But at what cost? Was I willing to lose the life I'd built, the people I loved, for this mission?

The question lingered, haunting me as I drifted into a restless sleep.

CHAPTER 19: THE TURNING POINT

The next week, Bill called a special meeting, saying he had something important to discuss. The air was thick with anticipation as we gathered in the small library room, our regular spot feeling almost sacred after months of meetings and discussions.

When Bill arrived, he was carrying a stack of papers, his expression serious. "I've been doing some digging," he began, passing the papers around the room. "What I found... it's unsettling."

The papers were filled with graphs, charts, and articles, outlining the influence of a handful of wealthy donors who controlled the funding for major political campaigns, media networks, and corporations. Bill explained how these donors wielded an almost unimaginable amount of power, shaping policies, controlling narratives, and silencing dissent.

"This is why we're here," he said, his voice steady but filled with conviction. "This is what we're fighting against. These people have control over everything we see, hear, and believe. They're the ones pulling the strings, making sure we stay in line."

The room was silent, everyone absorbing the weight of his words. I felt a surge of anger, a burning sense of injustice. These weren't just theories or suspicions anymore. This was real, tangible evidence of the power and corruption that had infected every corner of our society.

As the discussion continued, a sense of urgency filled the room.

We talked about ways to spread the word, to reach more people, to expose the truth that had been hidden for so long. Ideas flowed freely, each one building on the last, fueled by our shared anger and determination.

By the end of the night, we'd agreed to organize a town hall meeting, open to the entire community. This would be our chance to reach people on a larger scale, to share the evidence, to make them see what was really happening. It was a bold move, a step that could bring attention—both positive and negative—but we were ready. We were done hiding in the shadows, done whispering in small rooms.

As I drove home that night, a sense of purpose filled me, a determination that was almost overwhelming. This was no longer just a personal journey, a search for truth. It was a battle, a fight for justice, for freedom, for the right to know what was happening in our own country.

But as I pulled into the driveway, the glow of the porch light illuminating the quiet stillness of my home, a pang of guilt tugged at me. I thought of Lucy, of the distance that had grown between us, of the nights spent in silence, each of us lost in our own thoughts.

I was on a path that felt right, a path that I believed in with every fiber of my being. But at what cost? Was I willing to lose everything for this mission, this cause?

The question lingered, heavy and unresolved, as I walked into the house, the weight of my choices pressing down on me like a shadow that refused to fade.

CHAPTER 20: THE TOWN HALL

The town hall meeting was set for a Saturday evening in the largest venue we could manage—a local recreation center with rows of plastic chairs, a small stage, and a modest sound system. For weeks, we'd been planning this event, spreading the word, and preparing materials. Bill and I had even printed a small booklet filled with information, statistics, and questions meant to spark curiosity and encourage people to dig deeper.

As I helped set up the room that afternoon, a sense of nervous anticipation settled over me. This wasn't just a meeting, and it wasn't just another forum with familiar faces. This was our chance to reach a larger audience, to bring our message to people who might have never thought to question the world around them.

By the time the doors opened, a steady stream of people began to trickle in. Some were familiar faces from our group, others were strangers. There were older folks, families with young kids, young adults who looked curious and a little skeptical. Watching them take their seats, I felt a swell of pride. We'd brought them here; we'd given them a reason to question, to listen, to learn.

Bill and I took the stage as the room settled into a quiet hum. I gripped the microphone, feeling the weight of the moment. "Thank you all for coming tonight," I began, my voice steady but filled with a mixture of excitement and nerves. "We're here because we believe that truth is worth fighting for. We're here because we want to help each of you see what we've seen, to understand what's really going on behind the scenes."

As I spoke, I could see the faces in the crowd shifting, expressions softening from skepticism to interest. I told them about the things I'd discovered—the control of the media, the influence of corporations, the way politicians seemed to serve everyone but the people who elected them. I talked about my own journey, the months I'd spent searching, reading, questioning.

Then it was Bill's turn. He spoke about the power of community, about standing together to make a change. He shared the statistics we'd gathered, the stories of people who'd felt the same frustration, the same betrayal. His voice was calm but passionate, each word resonating with the crowd.

When we opened the floor for questions, hands shot up across the room. People asked about everything from political influence to the role of big money in campaigns. They shared their own experiences, their own frustrations, their own doubts. And with each question, I felt a growing sense of solidarity, a connection that went beyond words.

One man, an older gentleman with a weathered face, stood up and spoke in a voice filled with quiet determination. "I've been alive a long time," he said, his gaze sweeping the room. "I've seen a lot of things change, and not always for the better. But what you're doing here… it gives me hope. It makes me believe that maybe, just maybe, things can get better."

A wave of applause rippled through the room, and I felt a lump rise in my throat. This wasn't just a meeting. It was a movement. And as I looked around, I knew that we were all part of something bigger than ourselves.

Afterward, people came up to us, thanking us, shaking our hands, asking how they could get involved. Bill and I exchanged a look, a silent acknowledgment of the power of the moment. This was what we'd been working toward, the culmination of months of effort. We were no longer just a group of people with questions. We were leaders, guiding others toward the truth.

As I drove home that night, the pride I felt was tempered by a quiet ache. I'd achieved something I never thought possible, something that mattered. But at the same time, I couldn't shake the feeling that I'd left something behind, something I couldn't get back.

CHAPTER 21: THE COST OF CONVICTION

The success of the town hall sent ripples through our group. The next few weeks were filled with meetings, planning sessions, and discussions about how to build on the momentum we'd created. People were joining our group in record numbers, eager to learn, to share, to become part of the movement.

But as my involvement deepened, so did the distance between me and Lucy. We still shared a home, still went through the motions of everyday life, but there was an emptiness in our interactions, a hollow silence that grew with each passing day. She didn't ask about the meetings anymore, and I didn't offer any details. It was as if an unspoken truce had formed between us—a silent agreement to avoid the topic that had come to define my life.

One evening, as I was reviewing notes for an upcoming event, Lucy sat down across from me, her face drawn and pale. "Hank, we need to talk," she said, her voice barely above a whisper.

I looked up, sensing the weight of her words. "What's on your mind?"

She took a deep breath, her gaze steady but filled with a sadness that cut deep. "I can't do this anymore, Hank. I feel like… like I'm living with a stranger. You're so wrapped up in this world, in these meetings, these theories. It's like there's no room left for us, for the life we used to have."

"Lucy, I'm sorry," I said. "This isn't even about me anymore, it's so much bigger."

She looked away, her hands trembling. "I understand that,

Hank. But I need to know… is there still room for us in your life? Or have you given all of yourself to this movement?"

Her question hung in the air, heavy and unresolved. I wanted to reassure her, to tell her that she was still my priority, that our life together still mattered. But the words wouldn't come. The truth was, I didn't know if there was room for anything else in my life anymore. The movement had become my purpose, my mission, my reason for getting up every morning.

"I don't know, Lucy," I said finally, my voice barely above a whisper. "I don't know."

She nodded, a tear slipping down her cheek. "I just hope you find what you're looking for, Hank. I really do."

That night, as I lay in bed, I felt a sense of emptiness that was almost overwhelming. I was on a path that felt right, a path that I believed in with every fiber of my being. But at what cost? Was I willing to lose everything for this mission?

The question lingered, haunting me as I drifted into a restless sleep.

CHAPTER 22: BREAKING POINT

The weeks following that conversation with Lucy were some of the hardest I'd ever experienced. I threw myself into the movement, attending every meeting, leading every discussion, dedicating every spare moment to the cause. But no matter how much I accomplished, no matter how many people I reached, there was a hollow ache inside me, a quiet sense of loss that refused to fade.

One evening, Bill called a special meeting, saying he had important news to share. When I arrived, the room was buzzing with anticipation. People were murmuring, exchanging glances, speculating about what he might have to say.

Bill took the stage, his expression serious but excited. "I've been contacted by a journalist," he announced, his voice steady. "She wants to write a story about us, about what we're doing here. She believes in our cause, and she thinks our message deserves a wider audience."

A murmur of excitement rippled through the crowd. A journalist—a chance to reach even more people, to spread our message beyond our town, to make a real impact. This was the kind of exposure we'd dreamed of, a chance to bring our movement to a whole new level.

But as I looked around the room, a sense of unease settled over me. This was what we'd been working toward, what we'd fought for. But was I ready for it? Was I ready to take our message public, to put myself—and everyone else—in the spotlight?

After the meeting, Bill pulled me aside, his expression serious. "I need you to lead this, Hank. You're the face of this movement, the one people look up to. This is our chance to make a difference, but we need you to be at the forefront."

I nodded, feeling a mixture of pride and fear. This was my moment, the culmination of everything I'd worked for. But as I drove home that night, a quiet doubt gnawed at me. Was this really the path I wanted to take? Was I willing to expose myself, my life, my beliefs to the scrutiny of the public?

When I walked through the door, Lucy was waiting for me, her face pale and drawn. "Hank," she said, her voice trembling, "I heard about the journalist. Is it true? Are you really going to do this?"

I nodded, feeling a mixture of excitement and guilt. "Yes, Lucy. This is our chance. This is everything we've been working toward."

She looked away, her shoulders slumping. "I just hope you know what you're doing, Hank. I hope you don't lose yourself in the process."

Her words stayed with me long after she'd gone to bed. I was standing on the edge of something vast and uncertain, a journey that had no clear destination, no way back. I was searching for truth, for justice, for a purpose. But at what cost?

As I lay in bed, the weight of my choices pressed down on me, a shadow that refused to fade. I was on a path that felt right, but the question lingered, haunting me: was I willing to lose everything for this mission?

CHAPTER 23: IN THE SPOTLIGHT

The day the journalist arrived felt surreal. Her name was Sarah Martin, a young woman with sharp eyes and a notepad she never seemed to put down. She'd reached out to Bill after hearing about our group through mutual contacts, and she was intrigued by what we were doing—regular people, organizing on our own, pushing against what we saw as the boundaries of the establishment. Her presence was both thrilling and intimidating. This was our chance to get our message out to the world, to spread our truth beyond our community. But at the same time, I couldn't shake the feeling of exposure, like my life was under a microscope.

Sarah spent the afternoon with us, asking questions, recording our conversations. She wanted to know why we were doing this, what had driven us to question the status quo, to organize and push back. I told her about my own journey—the feeling of disillusionment, the nights spent searching for answers, the realization that so much of what we believed was built on carefully crafted narratives.

She nodded, her pen moving quickly across the page. "And what do you hope to accomplish?" she asked, looking up from her notepad, her gaze intense. "What's the ultimate goal?"

I paused, thinking carefully. "We want people to see the truth," I said finally. "We want them to question what they're told, to look beyond the surface. We want to create a world where people aren't just blindly following orders, where they're thinking for themselves."

She seemed satisfied with my answer, nodding as she jotted down more notes. But the question lingered in my mind. What was our ultimate goal? Was it just about awareness, or was there something deeper, something more fundamental that we were striving for?

When the interview was over, Sarah thanked us, promising to keep in touch. As she left, Bill turned to me, his face alight with excitement. "You did great, Hank," he said, clapping me on the shoulder. "This is going to be big. People are going to see what we're doing, and they're going to want to join us."

I nodded, feeling a swell of pride. But as I drove home that night, a quiet unease crept in. I'd shared so much of myself, so much of what I believed. And while it felt empowering, it also felt like I'd given something away—like I'd opened a door that couldn't be closed.

When I got home, Lucy was waiting for me, her face drawn and pale. "I heard you had the interview today," she said, her voice barely above a whisper.

"Yes," I said, my tone cautious. "It went well. I think this is really going to help us reach people."

She nodded, her eyes glistening with unshed tears. "I know this is what you really want, I'm Hank, I just don't know how much more I can handle."

CHAPTER 24: FRACTURED BONDS

In the days following the interview, the tension between Lucy and me grew heavier, like a shadow that lingered over every conversation, every moment of silence. We went about our routines, but there was a distance between us that felt insurmountable. She tried to be supportive, to pretend that everything was fine, but I could see the strain in her eyes, the quiet sorrow that seemed to deepen with each passing day.

One evening, as we sat down for dinner, Lucy looked at me, her face pale and drawn. "Hank," she said softly, "we need to talk."

I put down my fork, bracing myself. "What is it?"

She took a deep breath, her gaze steady but filled with a sadness that cut deep. "Hank, every day it feels like you're slipping further away, like this movement has taken over your life. I don't even know who you are anymore."

"Lucy, I'm sorry," I said, my voice breaking. "But this... this is important to me. I feel like I'm finally doing something that matters."

She shook her head, a tear slipping down her cheek. "I understand that, Hank. I really do. But what about us? What about the life we built together? I feel like I don't even recognize you anymore."

I looked away, unable to meet her gaze. The life we'd built—the quiet evenings, the shared moments, the dreams we'd once had—felt like a distant memory, something that belonged to a different time, a different person.

"Lucy, I don't know how to go back," I said finally, my voice barely above a whisper. "I've seen too much. I've learned things I can't unlearn."

She nodded, her face filled with resignation. "I just hope you find what you're looking for, Hank. I really do."

We sat in silence, the weight of her words pressing down on me like a leaden blanket. I knew I was on a path that felt right, a path that I believed in with every fiber of my being. But as I looked across the table at the woman I'd once shared my life with, I couldn't shake the feeling that I'd lost something precious, something that I couldn't get back.

CHAPTER 25: A MOMENT OF RECKONING

The article came out two weeks later, and the impact was immediate. People from neighboring towns began reaching out, wanting to learn more, to join our movement. Our meetings were packed, the energy in the room electric. It was everything we'd hoped for, a validation of our efforts, a sign that we were making a difference.

But as the excitement grew, so did the pressure. Bill and I were fielding calls from journalists, community leaders, people who wanted to collaborate, to turn our movement into something larger, more organized. We were no longer just a small group of concerned citizens. We were becoming a force, a presence that people couldn't ignore.

One evening, after a particularly intense meeting, I found myself alone in the parking lot, the night air cool and crisp. I leaned against my car, staring up at the stars, feeling a mixture of pride and exhaustion. I'd come so far, sacrificed so much. But as I stood there in the quiet darkness, a question gnawed at me: was it worth it?

I thought about Lucy, about the distance that had grown between us, the life we'd once shared that now felt like a distant memory. I thought about the nights spent in front of my computer, the hours of reading, questioning, digging for answers. I'd given so much of myself to this cause, poured every ounce of my energy into it. But in doing so, had I lost something even more important?

As I stood there, a wave of doubt washed over me, a deep, unsettling feeling that I'd been avoiding for months. Was I really making a difference, or was I just filling a void, a need for purpose that had grown too large to ignore?

The thought shook me to my core, and for the first time, I wondered if I was on the wrong path, if I'd sacrificed too much in pursuit of a truth that might never be found.

The next day, I woke up feeling hollow, a quiet ache in my chest that refused to fade. I went through the motions, attending meetings, answering calls, but the passion that had once fueled me felt distant, muted. I couldn't shake the feeling that I'd lost something precious, something I couldn't get back.

That evening, as I sat alone in the quiet of our living room, Lucy came in and sat beside me. She didn't say anything, didn't ask any questions. She simply took my hand, her presence a quiet comfort that I hadn't realized I'd missed.

For a long time, we sat in silence, the weight of unspoken words hanging between us. And in that silence, I felt a glimmer of something I thought I'd lost—a connection, a sense of belonging, a reminder of the life we'd once shared.

As the night wore on, I knew that I was at a crossroads, a moment of reckoning that would define everything that came next. I could continue down this path, pouring myself into a cause that felt larger than life. Or I could choose something different, something quieter, but no less meaningful.

In that moment, I realized that the choice was mine, and mine alone. And as I looked at Lucy, her face filled with quiet hope, I knew that whatever path I chose, it would be one that I could live with, one that honored the life we'd built together.

For the first time in months, I felt a sense of peace, a quiet certainty that no matter what came next, I would be okay. We would be okay.

CHAPTER 26: THE CROSSROADS

After that evening with Lucy, a quietness settled over me that I hadn't felt in a long time. I still attended meetings, still participated in the movement, but there was a shift in my heart. The relentless drive, the burning need to uncover every hidden truth, had softened, leaving behind a calm that allowed me to step back and see things with fresh eyes. The pursuit of truth had felt like my purpose, a mission that I couldn't let go of. But for the first time, I began to wonder if there was more to life than this endless search.

One afternoon, as I walked into our usual meeting space at the library, I felt a sense of detachment that was both strange and comforting. The familiar faces of my friends—Bill, Linda, Marcus, and others—greeted me warmly, but I sensed something different, as if I was observing from a distance, seeing the group as an outsider would.

Bill was leading the meeting, discussing plans for another town hall and an outreach project that would involve door-to-door conversations with our neighbors. The energy in the room was palpable, each person fueled by a desire to spread the message, to bring others into the fold.

But as I listened, I felt a strange disconnect, a sense of exhaustion that I hadn't noticed before. I couldn't help but wonder if our mission had become more about pushing a message than truly connecting with people. Was our goal to foster understanding, or had it become something else—something more about validation, about proving ourselves right?

The meeting ended with the usual enthusiasm, plans set, hands shaken, and as everyone left, Bill pulled me aside, his expression concerned.

"You've been quiet lately, Hank," he said, studying me. "Is everything all right?"

I nodded, managing a small smile. "Yeah, Bill. I'm just… thinking, I guess."

He looked at me, a flicker of understanding in his eyes. "You know, it's okay to step back sometimes. This work is important, but it's not everything. You've got a life outside of this, people who care about you. Don't lose sight of that."

His words struck a chord, and as I walked back to my car, I felt a sense of clarity beginning to take shape. I'd been so consumed by the movement, by the need to find answers, that I'd forgotten the simple truths that grounded my life—love, connection, the small joys that made each day worth living.

That night, as I lay in bed, Lucy's soft breathing beside me, I knew that I was standing at a crossroads. I could continue down this path, pushing for change, or I could choose something quieter, something that honored the life I'd built and the people I loved.

CHAPTER 27: LETTING GO

The next morning, I woke up with a sense of determination that had eluded me for months. I didn't know what the future held, but I knew that I needed to find balance, to reconnect with the life I'd once cherished. The search for truth was important, yes, but I'd come to understand that it wasn't everything. There were truths closer to home that mattered just as much, if not more.

That evening, I sat down with Lucy, feeling the weight of unspoken words between us. She looked at me, her expression a mixture of hope and caution.

"Lucy, I just want to say I'm sorry," I began, my voice steady but filled with emotion. "I know I've been… somewhere else these past months, and I know it's hurt you. I didn't realize how much I'd drifted away; how much I'd let this take over my life."

She reached across the table, taking my hand, her eyes softening. "I know, Hank. I know you believed in what you were doing, and I understand why. But I've missed you. I've missed *us*."

Her words brought a lump to my throat, and for a moment, I couldn't speak. I'd been so focused on the movement, on my mission, that I'd forgotten the simple beauty of the life we'd built together. The quiet moments, the shared laughter, the comfort of knowing that I wasn't alone.

"I think… I think I'm ready to step back," I said finally. "I still believe in the truth, in questioning things. But I don't want it to consume me. I want to be here, with you, with our life."

Lucy smiled, a tear slipping down her cheek as she squeezed my hand. "That's all I've ever wanted, Hank. Just to have you back."

The relief that washed over me was overwhelming, a weight lifting from my shoulders as I realized that I didn't have to choose between truth and love, between purpose and connection. I could have both, but only if I allowed myself the space to be fully present, to live a life that honored both my beliefs and my relationships.

CHAPTER 28: A NEW CHAPTER

In the weeks that followed, I found a new rhythm, a balance that allowed me to stay connected to the things I believed in while also cherishing the life I'd nearly lost. I still attended meetings, still participated in discussions, but I approached it all with a gentler, quieter perspective. I no longer felt the need to prove myself or to convince others of the "truth." Instead, I found value in simply listening, in sharing perspectives without judgment or expectation.

One evening, as I was finishing up some work in the garage, Bill stopped by, his expression thoughtful. "I heard you're stepping back a bit," he said, leaning against the workbench.

"Yeah," I replied, nodding. "I think I needed to find balance, to remember what's really important to me."

He looked at me, a hint of respect in his eyes. "That's not easy to do, Hank. I think you made the right choice. This work is important, but so is living a full life."

We stood in comfortable silence, both of us reflecting on the journey we'd shared. Bill had become more than just a friend; he was a mentor, someone who had guided me through some of the most challenging months of my life. And though our paths were diverging, I knew that the bond we'd formed would remain.

As he left, I felt a sense of closure, a quiet satisfaction in knowing that I was exactly where I needed to be. I wasn't giving up on the things I believed in, but I was choosing to approach them in a way that honored my life, my love, my sense of self.

Later that night, as Lucy and I sat on the porch, watching the sun dip below the horizon, I felt a peace that I hadn't known in a long time. We held hands, sitting in companionable silence, the quiet beauty of the moment filling me with a profound sense of gratitude.

"Thank you, Lucy," I whispered, my voice filled with emotion. "Thank you for being here, for staying with me through all of this."

She smiled, resting her head on my shoulder. "I'll always be here, Hank. As long as you're here with me."

In that moment, I knew that I had everything I needed. The truth was important, yes, but love, connection, and the simple joys of life were just as vital. I was no longer a man searching for answers; I was a man who had found peace, a man who had learned to let go.

And as the stars began to twinkle above us, I knew that this was the beginning of a new chapter—a chapter defined not by questions or missions, but by love, by presence, by a quiet, enduring truth that would carry me through whatever came next.